I Belong Special

Leader's and Parent's Guide

First Holy Communion Programme for a Child with Intellectual Disability

Cristina Gangemi MA
ibelongspecial@rpbooks.co.uk

redemptorist
publications

I Belong Special
First Holy Communion Programme
for a Child with Intellectual Disability

Published by **Redemptorist Publications**
Alphonsus House, Chawton, Hampshire, GU34 3HQ, UK
Tel. +44 (0)1420 88222, Fax. +44 (0)1420 88805
email rp@rpbooks.co.uk, www.rpbooks.co.uk

A registered charity limited by guarantee.
Registered in England 3261721.

Copyright © Redemptorist Publications, 2012

Text: Cristina Gangemi
The MEET and PSR processes have been designed and developed by Cristina Gangemi and are copyright to her MEET 2006 PSR 2011.

Reader: Elizabeth O'Brien

Illustrations © Finola Stack
Design: Eliana Thompson

First published: September 2012

ISBN 978-0-85231-402-9

All rights reserved. No part of this publication may be reproduced, stored in a retrieval system, or transmitted in any form or by any means, electronic, mechanical, photocopying, recording or otherwise, without prior permission in writing from Redemptorist Publications.

Redemptorist Publications is not responsible for the content of external websites mentioned in this publication. The inclusion of a website address should not be understood to be an endorsement of that website or the site's owners (or their products or services).

A CIP catalogue record for this book is available from the British Library.

Printed by Cedar Group, Romsey SO51 9J

redemptorist
publications

Dear Catechist, Parent or Carer

Welcome to *I Belong Special*! I would like to share a little with you about this wonderful resource. The ministry of a catechist is a true gift the Church, and many people all over the world give up their time to pass on the scripture stories, church teaching and their personal faith experiences.

The word "catechesis" comes from a Greek word used by Ss Paul and Luke, originating from two words: *Kata*: down, and *Echein*: to sound, re-sound or echo. Therefore, the catechist is a person who echoes down their faith to others. When we encounter the gift of a child with an intellectual disability, within our catechetical activities, the handing down may *seem* more challenging due to the varied communication skills that the child may have. We hope that this exciting resource, which draws on many of the techniques used in special education, will enable you to share God's love, the grace of reconciliation, and the beauty of receiving and belonging to the Body of Christ.

I Belong Special is a translation of the *I Belong* first communion programme. This means that I have looked at each chapter from *I Belong* and have translated the pages into a set of actions and images that can be used to mediate church teachings, practice and scripture, in a way that is both meaningful and accessible.

Everyday experience

This programme is based on everyday experiences, and encourages children and parents to find the deeper realities behind these experiences. This includes living together as a united Christian family where all are equal and where all belong, no matter what ability. *I Belong Special* has therefore been designed so that children with intellectual disabilities can be catechised alongside their peers, using the same programme.

Indeed, the *General Directory of Catechesis* states that people with disabilities are considered "particularly beloved by the Lord and the community" and suggests that "growth in our understanding of disability, along with progress in specialised pedagogy, makes it possible and desirable for all to have adequate catechesis." The *Directory* (No. 189) goes on to say that each child, through baptism, gains the right to catechesis and that for a disabled child "Programmes for catechesis should be personalised and should use modern pedagogical methods. They should be in the mainstream of parish life".

The welcome of children with intellectual disabilities within mainstream classes sits at the very heart of *I Belong Special*, although this resource can also be used on a one-to-one basis. The welcome into mainstream catechetical activities, however, is the most recommended option. *I Belong Special* is designed to make full use of your gifts as a catechist or carer, allowing everyone involved, simply and creatively, to explore the themes of the programme together. This is a journey to the sacraments, where children of all abilities can belong, where they can *receive,* but most importantly where they may *contribute*.

The use of scripture and sign language

Scripture is at the very heart of the *I Belong* programme and the children are offered the opportunity to explore their everyday realities, allowing them to be enriched through the words of the Bible. In the book you will therefore find the life experiences of children who use wheelchairs, communicate through sign, or who need visual cues in order to understand and process information. Indeed, in *I Belong Special*, we find Jesus and other people signing Makaton – a language of signs and symbols that mediates meaning.

The chapters encourage the children to become part of Catholic worship, explore the practices and symbols that they see in church, and understand their meaning and purpose. The Family Time page at the end of each chapter is designed to allow the whole family to share and pray together as they engage in trips to church, taking photographs and sharing meals. The Family Time section helps to make sense of the whole chapter, allowing the child to make a link between home, parish and school.

Communication

As the whole of *I Belong Special* is based on mediating and communicating faith to children with intellectual disabilities, it is important that, as the child's catechist, you feel part of the catechetical team. It will be very important to meet with fellow catechists and discuss how inclusive and welcoming sessions can be planned. Each session should allow the child to use their *I Belong Special* translation alongside peers. Regular meetings as a team will allow catechists to pray together, explore the themes of the sessions and decide how to echo down their meaning into the reality of *all* the children's lives. Meeting and praying together will model the community and communal activities which the children are invited to take part in. It will also give the team time to share any hopes and concerns that arise on the journey together.

Getting to know families will also be very important. All too often parents of disabled children experience social exclusion and isolation from mainstream activities. If we are truly a Eucharistic community there can be no outsiders. Every person, no matter what their ability, makes up the body of Christ, each according to their particular way of being. (This is based upon Canon 208 of Canon Law of the Catholic Church.) The community aspect of the Eucharist is never more powerful and evident than when we gather as a multi-ability catechetical group. Where children with disabilities *belong* to our parish and catechetical preparation, unique witness is given to one another and to the world. The welcome and equality, which is so central to the ministry of Christ, becomes the witness that we give. Communion and community is good news, not only for a chosen few… rather, it is a message of hope for all people and a *way to be* Christ's body and reveal God to others.

When catechising a child with an intellectual disability your main concern may be "How can I know they understand?", but it is important to keep in mind that there are indeed many forms of understanding and many ways to learn. It is the sharing and mediating that you do which allows the child's particular way of learning to become a moment of encounter with Christ and his Church.

Your own spiritual life

Knowledge and love are vitally important and can found in Bible and church teachings. They feed all that we do, putting us in touch with the words and actions of Jesus. These words echo into our lives and as such Jesus becomes our chief catechist. Your role as catechist is therefore to use all that Christ does, so that each child can encounter and experience that same glory of God that you have encountered in your own life.

I Belong Special has been designed to help you do just that. You do not need to be an expert in special education but you will need to take a little more time in preparation, for example photocopying, cutting and gluing. I can assure you that the results will be rewarding. As you catechise in this innovative way, you will experience the release of powerful insights from our children and, as such, you will be drawn into the very nature of God and the Eucharist. As you engage in catechesis, take time to pray and be with God. In this way, moments of prayerful encounter will guide your sharing, and you will know and feel the spirit of God stirring within you, leading you to explore "new ways of understanding" – of the heart as well as the mind.

I do hope that you will enjoy this creative and imaginative catechetical journey and that *I Belong Special* will lead you to discover that a "sacramental imagination" can be a source of working with images and actions, signs and symbols in a way that allows your own creativity to be an outward sign of God at work in your life.

May God bless, guide and inspire your sharing.

Cristina Gangemi

NOTES

Contents

Mediating catechesis — 8

The processes you will use — 12

A page-by-page directive — 15

Chapter

1. *In the name of the Father* — 17
2. *Lord, have mercy* — 23
3. *Celebrating our rescue* — 27
4. *God helps me get it right* — 33
5. *Glory to God in the highest* — 37
6. *The word of the Lord* — 39
7. *Bread to offer* — 43
8. *Fruit of the vine* — 49
9. *Do this in memory of me* — 53
10. *Body of Christ* — 57
11. *To love and to serve* — 61

Contacts — 62

MEDIATING CATECHESIS

What follows is a series of guidelines which will help you work alongside the child with intellectual disabilities. These are the structures and processes that you will need to adopt to ensure that the *I Belong Special* programme is effective. Please take time to read though and plan accordingly with your team.

Once you are familiar with the process, you will find it will become second nature. Alternatively you can book an *I Belong Special* training course for your parish or deanery. Email ibelongspecial@rpbooks.co.uk for more information.

The guidance has been designed as a series of questions and answers.

Questions you may ask yourself

What do I need to know before I begin to catechise a child with an intellectual disability?

The first thing you need to know is that the child whom you will catechise has been wonderfully and awesomely created (Psalm 139). As wonderful creations of God, all children have gifts to share. This means that you begin your journey by getting to know the child and their family, seeing them as a person with much to contribute. Please focus on their gifts: what they are *able* to do not what they are *unable* to do.

As soon as you have the request for support you should:
Meet with the child and parents and carers;
Reaffirm the fact that the child and family are welcome, and that they belong to the community;
Explore all that the child is able to do and, after this, what they may find challenging.

What are the creative ways of learning and understanding that were mentioned in the Introduction?

For a child with a learning disability, "visual language" is used to support learning and communication. This should not be too full of information, which may prove too much to process. You will see that the written word has been limited to a minimum, with the "visual" directing activities: images tell stories, symbols enable self-expression and allow questions to be answered. As well as characters communicating through Makaton sign language (see www.makaton.org for more information), you will also find Jesus signing in Makaton, showing that he seeks to communicate with all people.

Structure and continuity are vital when catechising a child with cognitive and intellectual disabilities. Rather than "teach", we try to "mediate information" by following a set process and structure. I have therefore devised a *process* for mediating and presenting the information from each page and it should be used for each session you share.

What structure and process should I use?

The **MEET** Process has been adapted for use within *I Belong Special*. The following is an outline of the **MEET** Process as an *I Belong Special* session plan.

Meet: Gather all the participants and welcome them, encourage them to communicate about their lives: who they have met/seen/shared time with. Play some soft music which enables them to relax and reflect. The music will add the audio cue that the session has begun; for children who are deaf you will use a visual cue.

Explain: Remaining as a group, explain the theme of the session (chapter) using different resources, language and process patterns (story bag, drama, music or symbolic activity).

Explore: Invite the children to move to a table-top activity, inviting the child/ren with intellectual disability to *explore* the theme in more depth. Alongside their peers using their *I Belong* book, they will use the *I Belong Special*. According to the abilities of the child you can share the whole chapter, or focus on whichever activity you feel explores the main message.

Transcend: After a suitable period of time, re-gather the group. Invite the children to share examples of the activities and pages completed in the book. It is vital that you include the child/ren with disability in this, encouraging them to express what they explored in the session, and what knowledge and experience they gained as a result. In this way, the children have all gained transcendent knowledge: at the end of the session, they have more experience of faith than they did when they began. A child who does not practise the spoken word can point to "emotion strips" (Happy/Sad/Sorry/Help) that are found in the book. Play some music to indicate the end of the session.

What process will I find on each page, which will help me mediate the session?
Each page of *I Belong Special* has the following "mediating process" **PSR** (Purpose, Share, Respond):
P: Every page has a *purpose*: this is the aim of the page and the message that it hopes to mediate;
S: Every page *shares* stories and theology: the story, words or imagery that help the child engage within the session and by which we seek to echo down faith stories, tradition and scripture;
R: This is where the child is invited to *respond*: each page asks the child to express and respond to what has been shared. For a child with an intellectual disability, the activities will enable them to respond as a result of what is actually seen and done.

What are the main mediating techniques I need to use?
Placement: Each page asks the child to use the technique of "placement" (adapted for use in *I Belong Special*). This is a tangible method of supporting reasoning skills and information-processing. It combines visual resources, visual spaces and audio/signed guidance, with physical movement and the symbolic placement of images (or a visit to a relevant place). The aim is to make a tangible, symbolic connection. For example, if you wish to use placement to help a child see that Jesus loves them:

Visual resources: You need a photograph of the child, a small heart shape, and an empty page that has space to stick an image on;
You tell/sign the child and physically move the heart and place it onto the photograph of the child;
You then symbolically place a small image of the face of Christ onto the heart and say/sign: "Jesus loves you".

Thus the placement becomes a symbolic and tangible representation of what you want to help the child to experience. Placement is used throughout the *I Belong Special* programme.

What is the best way to mediate the information in I Belong Special, *communicate and make full use of symbolic language?*

Mediating methods: It is important to systemise and organise your methods so that you invite the child to engage with the chapters and respond.

- Read the process for each page in the chapter, and choose which message you feel is most relevant and which pages the child will be able to do. You can always extend this.
- Obtain information about the skills and abilities of the child. Make sure that you have all the resources ready, copied, printed and cut out before the session begins. Be familiar with the activities and flow of the activity.
- Directions for tasks, the use of symbols, prompts and reinforcing activities, such as a church visit, must be planned and implemented in an organised and systematic manner, making the learning and the experience more predictable.
- Ensure that you communicate with participants in a way that meets their language, communication and processing skills.

Managing behaviour

People who have an intellectual disability can sometimes manifest challenging behaviour. This is not usually out of choice and can often mean that they are feeling frustrated or confused. It could also be a sign of their brain becoming over-processed. Generally, using structure, routine and symbolic activities ensures that themes and sessions become more accessible, and are less challenging. However, the following may help to keep the child feeling secure and motivated:

- Help the child to feel welcome within the group;
- Hold high expectations of behaviour and always stay calm;
- Use praise wherever possible: positive affirmation brings out positive behaviour;
- Touch can be difficult for some people with Autism: on meeting the person, hold your hand out for them to touch if they wish to – this will help you know if touch is challenging or not;
- Change can be challenging, especially for a person on the Autistic spectrum: preparing the person using photo cards or inviting them to come into the room before other participants may help the transition.

If you make changes to an environment or an activity aim to keep at least one feature constant, e.g. ensure that a piece of the furniture which you use within the session is kept in the same place.

- Stay calm but be firm, do not raise your voice as this may cause anxiety, just change the tone and rhythm of your words.
- Always remind people how you want the environment to be, especially when playing music – do not expect people to know instinctively.
- Your guidance will support and enhance positive interaction.
- Create a cordoned-off area in the room or a separate room for "time out". It *must not be* an area used for punishment or behaviour control.
- If inclusion in a large group proves too challenging and someone is becoming agitated or showing signs of over-processing, moving to a quieter place will enable them to become de-stimulated. It is important that they feel that it is their space.
- It is a good idea to have one piece of sensory equipment, such as a fibre-optic lamp, or a mirror or some soothing material in the quiet area.

All requirements surrounding the protection of vulnerable children must be applied.

Using symbols and making links to themes and concepts

By symbols we mean the use of images, or symbols supported by texts systems such as Widgit or Makaton (please see www.widgit.com and www.makaton.org for more information) or actual objects representing concepts or contextual realities.

Symbols are very effective when you wish to enhance understanding and cognitive processing. The symbol assists the reasoning process of a child or adult with an intellectual disability and helps them to have a tangible or visual connection to the spoken word. You can use real objects or graphics and you will see that this is what we use within the placement techniques of *I Belong Special*.

- Visual objects are always very useful for working with people of all abilities.
- When using symbols you should associate a symbol with a sign, gesture or written word.
- You can match a symbol or picture with an actual photograph or action (e.g. a visit to a church, or a baptismal font).
- You can match a symbol to a real-life object.
- You can match a symbol to the spoken word.
- You can link symbols with short, simple sentences or phrases.
- You can look for ways in which a person can respond by pointing, signing or using pointing sticks.
- Always look for the way in which you can recognise a yes/no answer and always acknowledge any movement.
- When you detect a response, try to answer, no matter how slight the movement may have been. Any movement, eye contact, or acknowledgement is a sign that the person is communicating or wishes to communicate with you.

THE PROCESSES YOU WILL USE TO MEDIATE THE JOURNEY

Each chapter of *I Belong Special* uses some common features and processes, which have been designed to help you mediate and follow the PSR process. What follows will help you to become familiar with these processes. You will need to have the *I Belong Special* book next to you as you go through the following directives, as it will allow you to become familiar with the book and with the features.

What are the main features of the I Belong Special programme that will help me catechise and mediate the programme?
You will need to become familiar with the following features.

Each chapter follows a colour code: The colours are first introduced on the contents page and you will see that each chapter has a matching colour border.

- Boxes for placing photographs of the child are usually in red.

- Boxes for ordering stories are in the order of blue, orange and green.

- Boxes for the child's response are usually in turquoise or blue. In this guide they will be called: R box.

- Lotto games are either in the colour of the chapter or in orange.

The scripture strip: Each Bible story has a "scripture strip" at the top of the page (e.g. page 4). This helps the child to identify that it is a Bible story as well as discovering if it is an Old Testament (OT) or a New Testament (NT) story. The aim is to help the child have a sense of the two parts of the Bible. The image of a Bible identifies the OT by a "G" on the left-hand page of the book, and arrows pointing upwards. The NT page holds an image of Christ. You will find a speech bubble which carries a message. You should always read this to the child. When you mediate these pages, it is a good idea to have a Bible close at hand so that the link can be made to a tangible object and to seeing it read at Mass.

The communication boxes: Underneath each scripture story you will find three boxes that will help you tell or put the story into order. You will do this by photocopying the main image of the Bible story. You should then cut out the characters or objects, according to how you think the child will be able to put them into some order. This process has been named the "Ordering Story Process" and it will appear in this guide as "follow the OSP". The scripture strip and communication boxes remain the same throughout the book so as to provide continuity of purpose, share and response (**PSR**).

Feeling strips: These strips are also red, so that the child is able to link them to his or her personal photograph and personal experience. The strips allow the child to point to and express his or her own feelings (e.g. page 20).

Image of Christ: We have used the same image of Jesus (e.g. page 70), right the way through. It is very important to use only this image of Christ and not to introduce new pictures as this could confuse and suggest that there are "different Jesuses".

The hand of God: Throughout the book (e.g. page 71) you will see hands that represent the movements of God. This is to assist the child to perceive visually the actions of God. The hands are: giving, helping, praising, blessing, holding and loving. It will be important that you highlight these for the child.

The lotto games: These allow the children to express themselves, make choices, explore the chapter and go over concepts. The lotto borders follow the colour of the chapter to ensure continuity and make links (e.g. page 11). To use the lotto game you will need to make a photocopy of each lotto game, cut out the squares and make matching symbol cards for the child to use; laminating the cards will mean that you can use them more than once and for more than one child.

Communication circles: The circles hold images in the centre (e.g. page 58). These images are always linked to the main theme. In symbolic language, placing a circle around an image implies that it belongs to something or someone. Therefore, you should invite the children to place relevant images, words or symbols into the circle, so that they can see that they are making personal choices and sharing personal information.

Some of the images show people signing in Makaton. It would be a good idea to learn the signs as well (please see www.abdn.ac.uk/kairos-forum).

This information will help you with your catechising; however, if you wish you may like to book an *I Belong Special* training day for your parish or deanery.

We also provide Kairos Makaton training days, which allow you to learn how to sign and how to implement it within catechesis. See the contacts page (page 62) for more information.

Sharing with and welcoming families

How do I welcome the parents of a disabled child?
Always make the parents and child welcome. Be aware that the parents may not be able to easily organise child care and may not be able to attend all sessions. It will be important to offer to take the sessions to them if necessary.

Use the same format as in the *I Belong Leader's Guide* so that the parents feel part of the community rather than people who need "special measures". You will need to discern what is best with sensitivity and friendship.

In your sharing with parents of a disabled child, always mention *I Belong Special* as part of the mainstream programme. It is as important as the main resource, and you can refer to it as a translation.

You should always be ready for parents who may have a disability. You can do this by providing a "welcome card" at registration and outreach stage. The card should ask about needs relating to the following: wheelchair access, British Sign Language, allergies, large print, Braille and any other needs. Never presume the abilities of parents: always be ready!

Allow parents to know and feel that they all belong to the group, and to the life and mission of the parish.

The *I Belong* liturgical services

The liturgical services should stay the same as in *I Belong*. However, I suggest that you could use the **MEET** process to give a continuity of structure within your sessions.

For example:
Meet the children and welcome them; play some music; say a prayer and show a symbol that represents prayer.
Explain and introduce the session with the suggested scripture story, using the *I Belong Special* images or movement to explain the story; or dramatise the story, maybe using a puppet show; say a few words, accompanied by symbols or objects, so as to explain your theme. You could also use the communication circle process (see above).
Explore: allow children to do an activity together or to have some sort of tactile engagement with the liturgy.
Transcend beyond all that they have experienced by gathering together again when all the children have prayed, sharing it with one another and then holding it all in a final prayer. Play some music; say the Our Father.

Chapters 1-11:
A PAGE-BY-PAGE DIRECTIVE

What now follows is the translation of *I Belong* into *I Belong Special*. This is done by giving page-by-page explanations of how to mediate and catechise the child with intellectual disability. The page numbers below all refer to *I Belong Special*.

Opening pages

First page of book
This page allows you to use photographs which will help the child to identify that it is a personal journey and to recognise who will be accompanying them on that journey.

Title page
This page allows the child to put the journey into perspective, gaining an idea of what they will be doing and why. It introduces the symbols of the Eucharist which they will see throughout the book and gives them a visual cue that they will be journeying towards the Eucharist with Jesus. Invite the child to stick their photograph in the given space as you gently explain the journey.

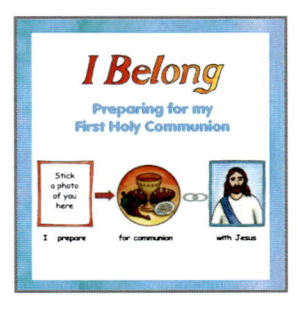

Contents page
This page allows the child to see the journey that they will be travelling on. It also gives you some small symbols to copy and cut out for future use if you need to.

From now on the translation will be presented from within the **PSR** process.

The journey begins…
You will need:
- A photograph of the child at their baptism.

P: This page visually takes a section of the road from the start of the book and allows the child to see that they are at the start of something. Its purpose is to allow the child to see that they are important to God and that from the moment of their baptism their journey of belonging to God has begun and that they make God happy.

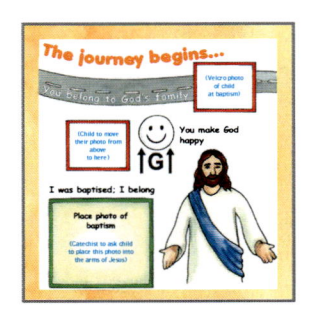

15

S: The page shares images and invites the child to use the process of "placement" to move into the arms of Christ.

R: The catechist should place the image of the child's baptism in the red box on the road. Invite the child to move the image and place it in the second box.
- Using simple sentences or signs, explain that the child belongs to God and that they make God happy.
- Help the child to say or sign, "I was baptised; I belong". If they cannot verbalise, then you should say the words slowly.
- Then ask "Who do you belong to?" Invite the child to place their photo into the arms of Christ. Praise and affirm the child.

When we go to church we...
You will need:
- Photocopies of the small symbols in the "tower" of the church; or photographs from the child's church.

P: This page has a picture of a church with doors wide open and welcoming. The church is divided into four boxes to form a lotto game for the response section. Its purpose is to assist in mediating the practices that we use when we are in the church.

S: The boxes share images of what we do, see and feel in church. Photographs will also give the child more scope for choice-making and observing.

R: Invite the child to respond by choosing images, bringing photos to the session, or maybe even visiting the church and matching photos or symbols to places. Use your imagination to gain a response from the child; you may not be able to rely upon verbal or written responses, so be prepared. Stick the choices in the R box.

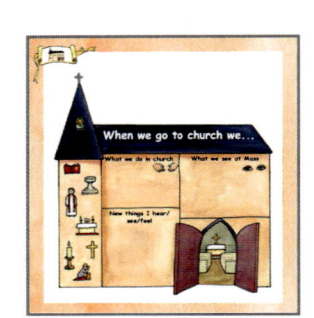

CHAPTER 1   IN THE NAME OF THE FATHER

Page 2
You will need:
- Photographs or images of objects or events that are named in the boxes on the page.

P: The purpose of this page is to build up knowledge and provide a glossary of relevant terms used in the book and in church.

S: The page shares teaching and symbols that are common to the Catholic Mass and tradition.

R: Invite the child to respond and communicate the links between what they hear, what they see and what they experience or will experience in the Mass. The words under the box will help you explain.

Page 3
You will need:
- Images of people that the child sees in church, including priest and servers.

P: This page helps the child know the community to which they belong.

S: Share the concept of belonging by linking it to real people.

R: Invite the child to respond by placing images of people who are important to them and whom they see in or know from church. Invite them to place an image of their particular church so as to make the link between image and reality.

Pages 4, 5 and 6
(All scripture stories will follow this process)
You will need:
- Photocopies of the pages.
- To follow the ordering story process (OSP) by cutting out the images so as to rebuild the story and make choices.

P: To help the child to know that the stories are shared from the Bible and to introduce the Bible to the child. All comes from God.

S: Explain the two parts of the Bible: Old Testament – before Jesus; and New Testament – with Jesus. Share the story and invite the child to become involved in that story. This will be done by telling the story slowly and simply or in a creative way (story bags, drama, etc.).

R: Give space for the child to make choices and express what God may be revealing to them.

Page 4
You will need:
- A Bible.
- A nature picture or object.

P: This page helps the child to reflect on the creative act of God. Show the Bible and explain that it holds importance for us as it tells us about God and Jesus. The phrase "word of God" may be difficult to explain, as children with an intellectual disability often think literally. They may therefore think that God only has one word and it may not link to any Bible story. You should therefore show the scripture strip and use the speech bubble to explain that the Bible helps us to know about God.

S: Share a story that helps the child experience a creative God. This could include looking at a flower or a nature picture. Point to the scripture strip, and communicate how Old Testament stories are about before Jesus was born and New Testament stories are about Jesus. The Bible helps us know how to live. We receive God's message. Following the OSP, prepare the story for the child to respond to.

R: Ask the child to choose any of the images you have cut out to order the story or to make a choice about God's creative act.

Page 5
You will need:
- A Bible.
- A small picture of Jesus from the *I Belong Special* book.

P: To present the New Testament and to show that it holds importance for us as it is where the Jesus story begins. It shows that Jesus is the beloved Son of God and is at God's heart.

S: Point to the picture of Jesus on the Bible. Tell child that this is a story about Jesus. You can link it to the section of the NT in the Bible. Share the story of the annunciation. You will need to keep the story very simple.
Suggested text:
"The angel told Mary, 'God loves you so much, please give us his Son.'
Mary said, 'If that is what God wants, I say Yes.'
Mary gave us Jesus from her love. Jesus is God's Son. God loves him. This simple story is from the New Testament and helps us know that Jesus was born and that God is his Father."

R: Following the OSP, invite the child to order the story or to communicate something about the story and about Jesus within God's story. Invite the child to place a small picture of Jesus in the heart shape so as to help the child understand Jesus in God's love.

Page 6
You will need:
- ■ To photocopy and cut out images in the story.
- ■ A Bible.
- ■ A photograph of the child.
- ■ A smiling face symbol.

P: This page begins to focus on the life story of Jesus. We must always keep in mind that any image of Jesus must be the same. You should use copies of the Jesus image from *I Belong Special*.

S: Point to the picture of Jesus on the Bible and explain the story of the baptism of Jesus. The words are in the boxes. Turn back to the page with the image of the child's baptism to communicate: "Just like you in God's family: it's great." After you have told the story, point to the smiling face in the scripture strip and communicate: "God is happy with Jesus."

R: You may like to invite the child to place a smiling face in the R box. By now you will have a better feel for the abilities of the child, so invite them to place an image of their own picture in the green box to make a link between God being happy with them as well as with Jesus.

Page 7
This page helps the child to link the waters of baptism to the holy water in the church. We suggest that you go for a visit to the church and let the child have a sensory experience of the water. Show reverence so as to highlight that it is special. Take a photograph of the holy water font, print and place it in the R box.

Page 8
You will need:
- ■ Photographs from the child's baptism.
- ■ Small picture of a smiling face (can be copied from book).
- ■ Small card with the child's name on.

P: This page presents the teachings of the Church concerning the relevance of personal baptism and membership of the family of God.

S: This page shares the unity that exists between the individual and others: it is about "being church". The child is invited to revisit their baptism and know that God is happy with them. This will be a very good reinforcement of previous pages. It is vital that the child has a sense of being a part of something, and begins to reinforce the community aspect of the Eucharistic journey. The left-hand column represents "now" and the right-hand represents "the past". This visual link helps the child to see that what happened on their baptism day is relevant to this journey they are making now.

R: The boxes on this page are designed for the child's response.

- The red box in the left-hand column invites the child to place a photo of themselves, as they are in the present.
- The "thought bubble" helps with memory: "I remember I was baptised".
- The blue box in the right-hand column invites the child to place a photo of their baptism.
- The first olive green box in the left-hand column shows a symbol of God (see above) and a speech bubble saying to the child: "You make me happy" – now, in the present. Invite the child to place a smiling face in the box, over the words.
- In the right-hand column the green box states: "The priest said you are God's special child". Invite the child to write or place their name (card) in the box. This shows how important their name is.
- The last box in the left-hand column has a symbol of God and also of a smiling face with the words: "I make God happy". Invite the child to move the name card they have placed in the previous box and place it into the "I make God happy" box. This shows that in the past and also in the present the child has continually been loved by God.
- The child should then be invited to move their own photo, from the box it is in, to the middle of the heart with the children's image. You should help the child see that they are part of a community of people that are loved by God and that they belong to a loving community.

Pages 9 and 10

I suggest that you make the words of the Our Father out of pictures. In the light of how you have been sharing with the child, discuss the best way to do this with fellow catechists.

Page 11

You will need:
- The name of the child, written down, and a small photograph.
- Matching lotto cards.

P: This page seeks to give the child a sense of the creative act of God in the creation of the world. God made a beautiful world where we can all live happily together. God wants us to look after the world and asks each one of us to play our part. This page holds a wonderful opportunity for you to affirm the child's important role within the parish community and within God's plan for the world.

S: The page allows you to share in the story of Adam that is found in *I Belong* and encourages you to help the child show how they can live as Jesus showed us how to live well. It encourages you to explore how, by living as Jesus did, we can live well and happily together.

R: The child is invited to match the actions that will help show that we live like Jesus did. You can extend this activity by finding alternative images of the same themes and sharing with the child, inviting them to match the images in the lotto game. I would also suggest that you seek to help the child explore how the images can be put into action; you may like to give the child one of the symbol cards to take home and focus on for the week.

Page 12 Family time

You will need:
- A photograph of the people with whom the child shares their life.
- Photocopies of matching symbol cards.
- To make a visit to the church and highlight practices during Mass and prayer.

P: This page seeks to bring together many of the themes and activities from the chapter. The aim is to help the child engage in the practices that they may see or do when they go to church.

S: Invite the child to pray with their family and loved ones in a creative way.

R: Invite the child to stick a photograph of their family in the appropriate box and pray together. This could be a photograph of the family/friends going to church together. When they go to church they should take the symbol cards that you have made with them. Invite the child to point to the matching actions as they recognise them. If this is difficult, the person with them should show how they match.

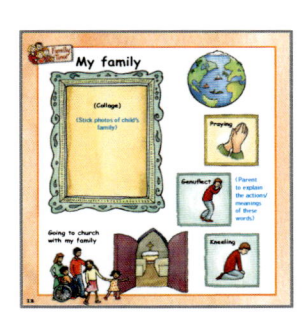

NOTES

CHAPTER 2   LORD, HAVE MERCY

If there is too much in this chapter to do, according to the needs and abilities of the child you are catechising, I would suggest that you use only one of the scripture stories.

Pages 14 and 15
You will need:
- A photograph of the child. You may like to use one from previous pages.
- Some images of good and bad choices that people make.

P: These pages seek to help the child place the concept of mercy into everyday experience. This has been made simple by linking forgiveness and a need for mercy into a concept of "making good or bad choices". The pages will help you accompany the child as they explore how we can seek God's mercy and how we do that by asking God and each other for forgiveness. According to the ability of the child, link this to the Penitential Act in the Mass.

S: The story of Katie and the kitten has been broken down into a simple format for you to share with the child. You can use the words in the box or just point to the pictures and say your own words, as long as they are simple and logical. The last box holds a space for the child to name the cat so as to engage in the story.

R: The whole of page 15 is a space for the child to respond in.
- Use the box to make a link between the good choices that Katie made in the story and a good choice that the child makes.
- Invite the child to place images of good and bad choices in the appropriate boxes. You could extend this by asking the people they share their lives with if there is something particular that they would like you to focus upon concerning good and bad choices. You should then ask the child to point to the heart that shows that they are loved.
- Do the same with the bad choice strip but carefully explain that God loves us always and God's love is there even when we make a bad choice.
- Point to the bad choice and, making a sad face, then point to the heart and say "God forgives us always, God loves us."
- Invite the child to place a photograph of themselves underneath the merciful hands of God and say or sign the words "please God". You should then say or sign "Have mercy on: _____ (name)."
- Invite the child to place their photograph in the R box where it states "I am loved". The whole box on mercy, at the bottom of page 15, will form a prayer card which can be copied and taken to church, as well as used in future chapters.

Page 16
You will need:
- A small picture of an apple.
- An image of Jesus (you can copy the image from the contents page).
- To following the OSP, you will need to cut the images into groups.

P: This page presents a story from the Old Testament and it is a good idea to highlight this for the child by pointing to the scripture strip and to the page marked "G". The message that comes from the Bible is that God gives us Jesus to help us make right choices. You can make this clear by placing an image of Jesus in the R box. You could also make links by showing the relevant part of a Bible. The story of Adam and Eve is a little different from that in the *I Belong* book. The aim of the story reinforces making good and bad choices.

S: The story of Adam and Eve has been simplified for you to share with the child. We have removed the words from the book so that the child is able to focus on the images. Suggested text:
"Adam and Eve lived in a beautiful garden. God said 'Do not eat the apples from the big tree.' A bad snake was on the tree; it said 'Eat the apple.' Adam and Eve ate the apple. They made a bad choice. They were worried and God was sad. Their bad choice made people sad but God sent Jesus to give everyone hope."
You may need to break this down even more according to the needs of the child.

R: Following the OSP, invite the child to make comments, order images and communicate feelings.

Page 17
You will need:
- Two images of someone showing forgiveness.

P: This page helps you to share the story of the prodigal son and begin to move towards a concept of penitence and forgiveness. This page has been designed to allow the child to follow the story from *I Belong* by "reading the images".

S: The story has been placed into boxes to give you an order for telling the story. The idea is that the father's love is present at the start and at the end of the story. The imagery in between continues the story but also builds upon the work that has been done on making good and bad choices. The focus is on the fact that we are always loved and that when we make a bad choice it affects others.

R: Invite the child to choose between images of forgiveness. Point to the speech bubble and say "Jesus says: 'Forgive'." You should then invite the child to place their chosen image of forgiveness into the R box.

Page 18
You will need:
- Some images of food.

This page is for the child to be creative and to fill the table ready for the party. Find and cut out images of food and drink from a magazine and encourage them to engage in a cutting-and-sticking exercise. In this way the child is making choices about what they would give to someone who has been forgiven and will bring the party and celebratory act of forgiveness into their own experience and action.

Page 19
You will need:
- A photocopy of the strip of choices at the bottom of the page.

P: This page allows the child to bring all of the sharing from the previous activities into one place. It also locates the act of mercy, asking forgiveness and being forgiven, within the liturgical action of the Mass.

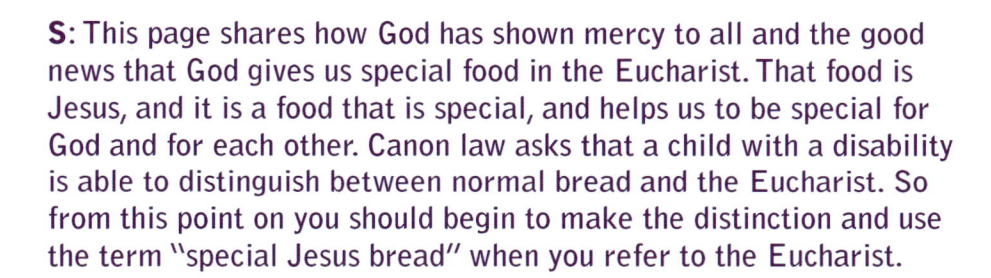

S: This page shares how God has shown mercy to all and the good news that God gives us special food in the Eucharist. That food is Jesus, and it is a food that is special, and helps us to be special for God and for each other. Canon law asks that a child with a disability is able to distinguish between normal bread and the Eucharist. So from this point on you should begin to make the distinction and use the term "special Jesus bread" when you refer to the Eucharist.

R: You should enable the child to make two responses on this page. First, encourage the child to point to the "bad choice" and then together look at the box with the special Jesus bread and say/sign or listen to the words "Lord, have mercy". Second, invite the child to place images of good choices into the heart shape that represents God's heart and assure them of God's loving heart receiving their good choices. You can extend this by using images of good or bad choices that they may have named during the session or you can use the images in the strip below the heart. Try to link this action to the Mass, using the mercy prayer card from page 15; encourage the child to take it to Mass with them and hold it up at the appropriate time.

Pages 20 and 21
You will need:
- To point to or copy feeling symbols.

P: Both pages invite the child to identify personal feelings and to explore the difference in emotions when they make a good or bad choice. This page seeks to locate the work of the whole chapter within the personal experience of the child.

S: The pages give an image of a child making a good and a bad choice, and invite the child to point to a feeling strip that shows what their feelings are or would be.

R: Invite the child to look at the picture and to point to the emotion that they would feel if they hurt or were kind to someone. These pages are fairly self-explanatory but you may want to extend the activity by inviting the child to express some of the choices they may have named in the chapter or may wish to name now that you have arrived at the end.

Page 22 *Family time*
This page should be left to the creativity of the family and loved ones. The idea is that the family fill the page with ways in which they show how they want to make the good choice of loving God.

CHAPTER 3   CELEBRATING OUR RESCUE

If there is too much in this chapter to do, according to the needs and abilities of the child you are catechising, I would suggest that you use only one of the scripture stories.

Page 24

Based on what you have learned from the child, about how they communicate and learn, use your creativity and invite the child to build a picture that reflects reconciliation.

Page 25

P: This page is designed to help the child reflect upon everyday experiences, and the concepts of danger and rescue.

S: The page shows images of children in a situation that is dangerous and one that is safe. The aim of the page is to invite the child to share feelings about the two situations and to be able to show the difference between the two. Invite the child, one image at a time, to look at the pictures and to respond to each situation independently.

R: Invite the child to point to the feeling strip and show how the boy in the wheelchair would feel. Invite them to also comment on how the child being saved would feel.

Page 26

Based on what you have learned from the child about how they communicate and learn, use your creativity and invite the child to build an image that reflects "rescue". NB You will need to be sensitive in the choices you make for this page. Please be careful not to use an image that may introduce fear into an activity that the child may have to engage in. You can use the scenario from page 25 if you need to.

Page 27
You will need:
- To follow the OSP.

P: Accompanying the *I Belong* book, this page tells the Old Testament story of Daniel and the lions. The aim for this page is to help the child to know that within a concept of being rescued, God saves.

S: The page presents the story of Daniel, shortened to help you share it with the child. Suggested text:
"Daniel was a good man. He prayed to God. The king and some men were angry with Daniel. They did not know God. The king threw Daniel into a pit with some lions. Daniel made friends with the lions. He was not in danger because he trusted God and God saved him. The king was amazed and he believed in God as well."

R: Following the OSP invite the child to interact with the story. Use the empty R box to encourage the child to give an example of how they feel God with them; or, to extend, how God saves them.

Page 28
You will need:
- To make a copy of the page and cut out an image of the small lamb on the cliff.

P: This page helps the child link the caring nature of a shepherd to the way in which God cares. The way in which God cares for us is found in the words and actions of Christ.

S: The page shares a story that Jesus told and also shows how Jesus uses storytelling to help people understand realities of God. The story should be shared in the following way:
"A shepherd had a lot of sheep. One of the sheep was in danger. The shepherd saved him and brought him back home."
According to the skills of the child, you can extend this activity by referring back to their previous work on being saved. This page, however, begins to introduce the word "rescue" and the following pages aim to help the child to understand its context.

R: Invite the child to place the photocopied image of the lamb into the appropriate gap that has been left among the sheep. Following the OSP, invite the child to order the story and/or fill the R box with personal emotions or response to the story. By this stage you should be familiar with the abilities of the child and be able to gauge how they might interact with the story. For this reason the boxes have been left empty.

Page 29

Using the skills of the child and your own creativity, invite the child to decorate this page and make it appear celebratory. You can cut and stick, use symbols or just colour.

Page 30
You will need:
- Images of good and bad choices that may be relevant to the child's life.

P: This page allows the child to reflect upon the choices that they have to make and what they need to help them make changes for the best.

S: Encourage the child to focus on their own personal experience. This page is almost all "Response"; however, there are some subtle clues to help the child use the feeling faces in the box. Encourage the child to point to feelings in boxes.

R: The R box should enable the child to express themselves. Using images you have gathered from magazines (or symbols), invite the child to fill the choice boxes. The choices will be put into the empty boxes; the feelings and needs boxes are there to help the child identify what they need in life and what they feel about life. The child signing sorry/sad face will help the child make the distinction between positive and negative actions.

Page 31
You will need:
- Photographs of parish celebrations.

P: This page begins to make links between sin, the need for rescue and church teachings on reconciliation. The image on the page is linked to the concept of road and journey which the child has experienced at the start of the programme. The image reflects the movement from a concept to an action.

S: The page shares church teachings concerning the process of the sacrament of reconciliation. The images along the road will help you to share with the child, helping them to see that when they make bad choices, it affects others. The next step on the journey shows that there is somewhere they can go to say sorry.

R: Here you should help the child understand that when we say sorry and are forgiven it is a time to celebrate. We say thank you for being forgiven. The celebration takes place in church. The space on the church should be filled with photographs of parish celebrations or special Masses or images that the child may choose to use.

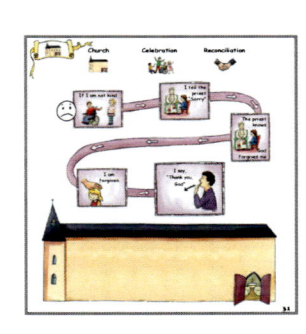

Page 32

You will need:

- To chat with the child's family and school, inviting them to tell you what they feel the child might do that is negative.
- Depending on the skills of the child, to invite them to make choices from previous pages and collect images that they identify as bad choices.

P: This page gives space for the child to reflect personally on the bad choices that they want to be forgiven for. You should help the child see how a celebration, a special time with the priest, can assist this process.

S: At the top of the page are the words "God always helps us" – this page is filled with links that should be highlighted in your sharing. The images in the boxes show how the helping hand of God is part of the process of forgiveness. The page also helps to show how going to spend time with the priest to tell him about making bad choices and being sorry is also part of that journey. The image of hands being shaken is a common symbol for reconciliation and friendship, and so it shows how the process of asking for forgiveness ends in reconciliation. The "thumbs up" sign, the child signing "thank you" and the words "It's good to be together: reconciled" will help you to join the links on the page and share faith with the child.

R: Show the child a series of bad choices; these may include suggestions from loved ones or anything that they have chosen to be forgiven for. Invite the child to place choices in the R box. The blessing hand of God will help the child see that forgiveness is a good experience and an action of God.

Page 33

You will need:

- To make a photocopy of the lotto game.
- To cut the pictures into matching cards.

P: This lotto game aims to help the child identify the concept of hope and link it to concepts throughout the chapter.

S: The game shares words that may help the reflection: the top row is the journey of forgiveness, the bottom is about the feelings that come with forgiveness and hope. The helping and giving hands of God will reflect the way in which God gives hope.

R: Invite the child to match images so as to consolidate all that they have experienced in the chapter so far. Invite them to point to the feeling strip to express how each card may make them feel.

Page 34 *Family time*

Encourage the family, carers or friends to make a visit to their church. You may like to accompany them and let them visit the reconciliation room so that the child can become familiar with it as a place they will visit in the future. Invite them to explore the space and take a photograph. When they are at home they can stick the photograph in the red box. The family can make links with the room and how it is a place to make good choices. The R box should contain a photograph of the child thanking God and making good choices. This will form a thank you card.

NOTES

CHAPTER 4   GOD HELPS ME GET IT RIGHT

Page 36

You will need:
- To photocopy the page or draw a line from the appropriate box to the choice of the child.

P: This page aims to identify everyday situations that may prove to be challenging in the life experience of the child. You should help the child to reflect upon the concept of challenge and rescue, which is a theme that is threaded throughout the chapter.

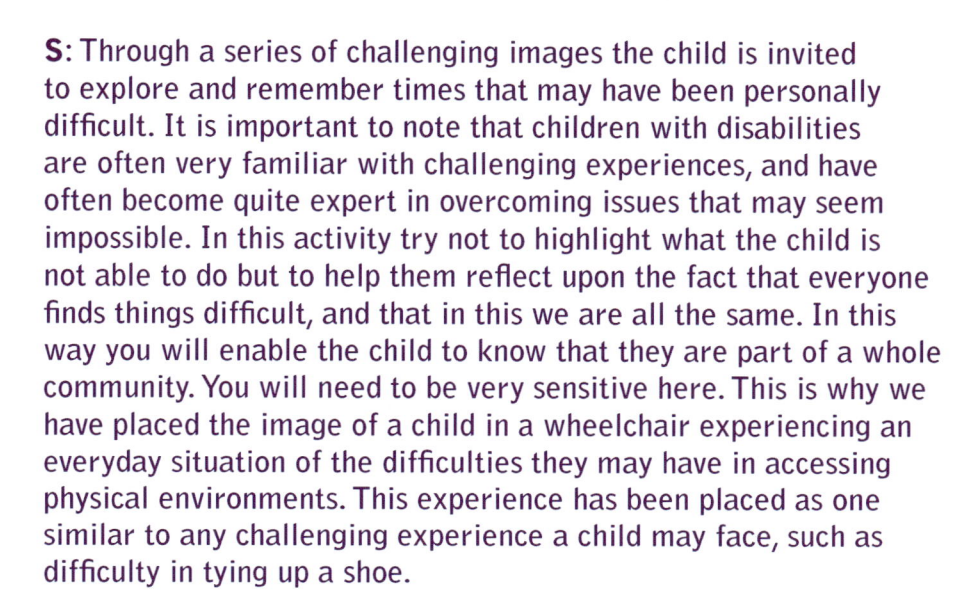

S: Through a series of challenging images the child is invited to explore and remember times that may have been personally difficult. It is important to note that children with disabilities are often very familiar with challenging experiences, and have often become quite expert in overcoming issues that may seem impossible. In this activity try not to highlight what the child is not able to do but to help them reflect upon the fact that everyone finds things difficult, and that in this we are all the same. In this way you will enable the child to know that they are part of a whole community. You will need to be very sensitive here. This is why we have placed the image of a child in a wheelchair experiencing an everyday situation of the difficulties they may have in accessing physical environments. This experience has been placed as one similar to any challenging experience a child may face, such as difficulty in tying up a shoe.

R: You should encourage the child to choose a difficult situation and to record their choice in the box. We have also given you a space for the child to express who has helped them. The aim here is to introduce a concept of rescue and a move from negative to positive by using the term "It's ok now", which the child will encounter on the next page.

Page 37

P: The purpose of this page is to visually assist the child to "see solutions" to the possible challenges that are visible on page 36.

S: The images on the page assist the child to reflect upon the concept of trust and assistance. Encourage the child to explore or observe how people trust others and are helped by others. Depending on the skills of the child you can extend this activity by sharing with the child how trust and help can allow them heightened self-esteem. This page shares images of things getting better.

R: Following the same process as page 36, allow the child to make choices of people getting things right. As the child uses the R box say the words "It's ok now".

Page 38
You will need:
- To follow OSP and simplify the story.

P: This page seeks to show how, through recognition of sin, an encounter with Christ can make things better. The page introduces the story of Zacchaeus and the difference that Jesus made to his life. Meeting with Jesus helped him to get things right.

S: The page shares the journey that Zacchaeus travels on, as he examines his conscience and desires to change his ways. The personal encounter with Jesus and the way in which Jesus chooses to be with Zacchaeus are told in a series of six self-explanatory images. The story shows the difference that believing in Jesus can make, no matter who we are. An important feature to highlight for the child is that Zacchaeus was a short man and that Jesus wanted to be with him no matter what. Jesus did not notice any difference; in fact he chose him deliberately to be an important witness in his ministry. The words for the story could be:
"Zacchaeus was a short man. He did not make friends. Jesus came to town. Zacchaeus climbed a tree to see Jesus. Jesus said, 'Come down.' Jesus wanted to eat with Zacchaeus. Zacchaeus changed and made friends with everyone."

R: Based on the skills of the child and with the knowledge you have of the child's communication skills, invite the child to make a response to the story and represent it in the R box.

Page 39
This page is for the child to respond to the story. Invite the child to identify when Zacchaeus made the good choice. The child is given the choice of identifying when Zacchaeus made a good choice, either before or after his encounter with Christ. Enable the child to make their mark in the appropriate box.

Page 40
You will need:
- A small photograph of the child.

This page is a page of celebration and allows the child to share in Zacchaeus' joy and transformation. You should invite the child to place their photograph at the table, allowing them to choose to be with Jesus and Zacchaeus. The sign of "It's ok now" will allow the child to be part of the experience of making a good choice. This will help them to prepare for their sacrament of reconciliation.

Page 41
You will need:
- A small photograph of the child.

P: The purpose of this page is to help the child to prepare for the sacrament of reconciliation and identify how sharing with the priest is the same as sharing with Jesus, and how together they make things better when we show sorrow for making a bad choice.

S: The page shares, in comic-strip form, what happens when a child goes to the sacrament of reconciliation. The child is asked to experience how making a bad choice, a sin, is wrong. The image of the child signing "sorry" should encourage the child to see that we need to show when we have done something wrong. The "thumbs up" helps the child to identify that showing sorrow is good. This is reinforced by the three boxes that tell the story of the encounter with the priest who stands as the person of Christ. Gently explain the pictures to the child; the simple words will help you.

R: The last two boxes on the page invite the child to say whether or not they show that they are sorry. You should invite the child to place their photograph in the box that asks them to say "yes" to being sorry, and then finally to stick their photograph permanently in the box that states that they are sorry. This is the child's way of expressing contrition and will form the act of contrition in preparation for the sacrament of reconciliation.

Page 42
This page is purely for the child to express themselves, and to make a page of bad choices. They will bring this page when they receive the sacrament of reconciliation. This page should be photocopied and given to the child to take to the sacrament.

Page 43
You will need:
- A photocopy of a completed page 42.
- The priest will need a bin and to use the child's *I Belong Special* book pages 42 and 43.

P: The purpose of this page is to prepare the child for the sacrament of reconciliation and provide them with a form of expression that will assist them before, during and after the sacrament. This page is extremely important for a child who does not use the spoken word.

35

S: The images on the page repeat those from previous pages. The page is divided into three rows. Row one identifies what should be done before the sacrament; row two helps the child to know what happens during the sacrament; and row three gives the child information about what it is like after they have received the sacrament.

R: Before the sacrament, invite the child to look at the picture of the priest. Prepare the child for the fact that that they will share bad choices with the priest and with God.
- Invite them to stick one bad choice into the R box in row one.
- Row two should be used by the priest during the sacrament, sitting with the child and sharing this page.
- The priest should point to the bad choices that have been recorded, either from page 42 or page 43.
- The priest should point to the symbol of "Sorry, God", and ask the child to do the same. Based on the skills of the child you could extend this by inviting the child to share about some of the choices they have made.
- The priest should then take the "Sorry" card, which is a copy of page 42, rip it up, put it in a bin and point to the box where the priest is signing "It's ok now".
- The priest should repeat this sign "It's ok now" to the child. Following the sacrament you should encourage the child to join their hands and pray to God. The R box at the bottom of the page will help you.

Page 44 *Family time*
Encourage the family and loved ones to support the child by inviting them to place a picture of themselves, on the day that they receive the sacrament of reconciliation. The purple box should show a photograph of them on that day and the R box should be left to the creativity of child and family.

CHAPTER 5   GLORY TO GOD IN THE HIGHEST

Page 46

P: This page invites the child to choose an everyday experience that is a little bit special and that has a sense of achievement attached to it. The child is invited to decide which one they like the best.

S: The page shares the story of a boy who has done well at a football match and a girl who is delighted as she watches the fireworks. You should take time, based on all you know about the child, to communicate about these different situations.

R: The child is invited to point to the experience that they felt was the most enjoyable. This page is all about inviting the child to make positive, personal choices.

Page 47
You will need:
- To photocopy the lotto grid and make individual matching cards.
- Images for which we give "Glory to God".

P: This lotto game helps the child to recognise the positive gifts that God gives us. Through these gifts we give glory to God.

S: The images that reflect the gifts of God are things that we want to say thank you for. We give glory to God. The lotto game is divided into three emotional spheres: Excited, Calm and Happy.

R: Invite the child to match images and to point to emotions that they may feel are linked to each image. Invite the child to choose from images you have brought and to place them in the empty lotto box. Invite the child to express their feelings.

Page 48
You will need:
- To follow the OSP.

P: This page presents a story from the Old Testament that retells the moment in which God makes himself known to Moses, and advises Moses that God has something important for him to do. This story aims to help the child understand that God is very important and the "praising hands" help reinforce this.

S: Suggested simplified words for this story:
"Moses was a special man. God called him. Moses saw a bush burn. A loud voice said 'I am God.' Moses praised God. God said 'Keep my people safe'."

R: Use the cut-out pictures to allow the child to order the story. Finish this activity by telling the child that God's "giving hand" sent someone special.

Page 49
You will need:
- To follow the OSP.

P: The purpose of this page is to allow the child to make the connection between God being revealed as God and as Jesus.

S: The story of the nativity allows you to use the term "Glory to God" and to decorate the page in a way that celebrates the arrival of Christ in the world. The simplified words for this story should be: "God gives us Jesus. We thank God. We say 'glory'."

R: Invite the child to order the story or, depending on the skills of the child, to talk about the nativity if they are able to. On both pages 48 and 49 giving glory to God is the central action to communicate to the child.

Page 50
You will need:
- A collection of images from your church of people praising and giving glory to God.

R: This page is all response and we would invite you to allow the child to fill the church with images of people praising and glorifying God. The aim is to facilitate a visual understanding of the celebratory nature of a community gathered.

Page 51
You will need:
- A collection of images that reflect the words in the lotto grid.

R: Invite the child to match their chosen image to the correct word. You will notice that there is one empty box. This is for the child to identify one particular thing for which they praise God.

Page 52 *Family time*
P: This page invites the family to recognise how giving "Glory to God" does occur in the Mass.

S: The page shows how "Glory to God" occurs when the child witnesses the Eucharist being held up for us all.

R: The empty R box should form a space for the family to create a thank you card. Encourage the family to make a photocopy of this thank you card and ensure that the child brings this to church so as to thank God for the community in which they belong.

CHAPTER 6   THE WORD OF THE LORD

Page 54
You will need:
- To follow the OSP.

P: The purpose of this page is to allow the child to recall and remember some Bible stories that they may have experienced or that they may like. Where this is not possible, you should bring some simple images of stories from the Bible for the child to choose from.

S: Following the way that we have simplified stories in previous chapters, share the story with the child.

R: Allow the child to order the story and encourage them to use the R box for their own personal favourite story.

Page 55
You will need:
- A photograph of the Gospel being read by the parish priest or deacon.

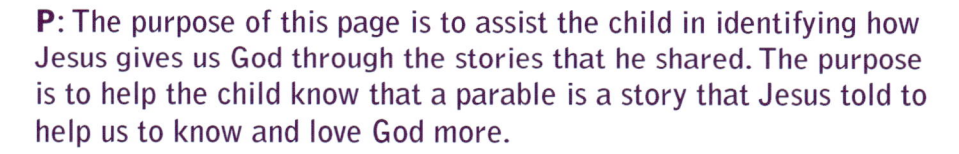

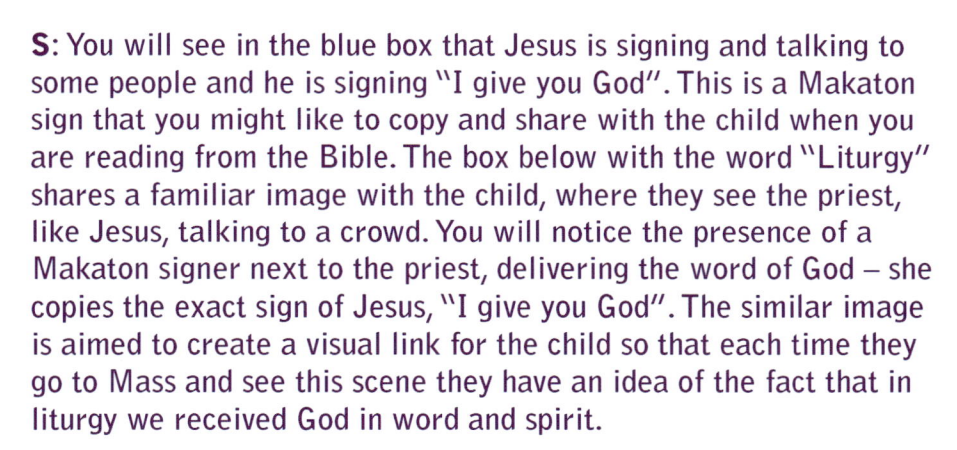

P: The purpose of this page is to assist the child in identifying how Jesus gives us God through the stories that he shared. The purpose is to help the child know that a parable is a story that Jesus told to help us to know and love God more.

S: You will see in the blue box that Jesus is signing and talking to some people and he is signing "I give you God". This is a Makaton sign that you might like to copy and share with the child when you are reading from the Bible. The box below with the word "Liturgy" shares a familiar image with the child, where they see the priest, like Jesus, talking to a crowd. You will notice the presence of a Makaton signer next to the priest, delivering the word of God – she copies the exact sign of Jesus, "I give you God". The similar image is aimed to create a visual link for the child so that each time they go to Mass and see this scene they have an idea of the fact that in liturgy we received God in word and spirit.

R: Invite the child to place an image of their own priest or deacon reading the Gospel and help them make the connection to all the images.

Page 56
You will need:
- ■ A collection of images or symbols of emotions and possible messages that children might receive when they receive help or when they give help.

P: The purpose of this page is to allow the child to fill the circle with anything they want, in a way that expresses what they feel when they receive something.

S: Using the process of circle communication this page shows a child with his hands open, ready to receive from God and from others. This is beginning to share the concept of scripture being given and the word being received. The feeling strip allows the child to identify their feelings as they receive the word of God.

R: Invite the child to fill the circle with images of objects and people that help them. Try to extend this by asking the child to share how they feel when they receive something or how they feel when they need something but do not receive it. You can use the feeling strip to help you.

Page 57
You will need:
- ■ To follow the OSP.

P: This page gives the story of Samuel and how he received a message from God, when he was called to serve God.

S: The story shows Samuel in the process of being called by God. The words for the story could be:
"Samuel was asleep. God called his name three times. Samuel was not sure it was God calling. After the third call, Samuel said 'Yes, Lord, I am ready.' Samuel received God's word."

R: The three empty boxes will help the child order the story. Your focus must be on receiving God's word for a purpose.

Page 58
You will need:
- ■ A collection of images or symbols of emotions and possible messages that children might receive when they share in the word of God.
- ■ A Bible and a picture of a gift or smiling face (you have many to copy from in this book).

P: This page invites the child to record how they feel when they receive the word of God.

S: Using the process of circle communication the activities on this page should be linked to those of page 56. The page shows an image of a Bible, from which we read the story of Samuel and give the word of God to others. Use this page to explore the story of Samuel further. You can enhance this by placing a picture or a symbol of a gift, or a smiling face into the Bible. Then open the Bible, take out the symbol and give it to the child. Say the words: "Like Samuel, receive a gift from God; receive God's stories." Your focus must be on receiving a message from God for a purpose. Fill the circle with images from the story, or of emotions that the child may have when they feel called by God or when they have a message to give.

R: Invite the child to fill the circle with whatever they choose from the images or symbols. Encourage the child to express how they feel when they receive a message from God or when they receive stories about Jesus.

Pages 59, 60 and 61

The following three pages aim to help you to explain the concept of Jesus as God's messenger, a gift from God, and that Jesus is the Word of God. For a child with intellectual disabilities, who may process information literally, a person cannot be a word. Use these pages to help the child process how God gives Jesus, and how Jesus gives us, God through his stories and actions.

Page 59

P: This page is purely catechetical and aims to show that Jesus is given to the child as a gift. It should link to the action where you gave the child a gift from the Bible on page 58. This page shows how God gives us Jesus as a baby and as a man.

S: It is important to help the child see that the baby that is given is the same person who grows up. The image of the child with his arms open is to be linked to the child receiving in the circle communication activities where the child has recorded "receiving". Help the child to make the link.

Page 60

You will need:
- Resources to decorate the page, with some glue for cutting and sticking.
- A copy of the image of the baby Jesus, cut out, from page 59.

P: This page is to help the child consolidate the fact that the nativity story is where the story of Jesus' life begins and that Jesus was a gift. This page invites the child to identify the fact that Jesus carries/gives the word of God to others.

S: The page shares how Jesus was born in the glory of the night, how he is the Word of God (speaks for God) and how God keeps his promise through Christ. The image of the empty cradle is ready for the child to place an image of a gift. The empty farmyard could be a place for the child to express their knowledge of the nativity story or to show how they understand the baby Jesus to be a gift.

R: Invite the child to stick an image of the baby Jesus, a Bible or indeed an image of their choice in the empty cradle. You can extend this by inviting the child to communicate how they feel Jesus is a gift from God.

Page 61
You will need:
- A photograph of the child.

P: This page helps the child to know that the Gospel is "Jesus telling stories about God".

S: The image of the large Bible has Jesus at the very centre of it. In the image Jesus is telling stories to people and they are receiving his stories. The image links to those on page 55 and will therefore be familiar to the child. The praying hands will help you explain that the stories are special and help us to pray.

R: Invite the child to place a photo of themselves in with the group listening to Jesus, or you could write the child's name. In this way they will be able to link their personal experience of receiving the stories from the Bible to watching as the Gospel is read and signed in church. This can then be linked with the image on the Bible and with receiving the word of Jesus. They are invited to be with Jesus.

Page 62 *Family time*
You will need:
- Images that link to the actions of the children on this page.

P: This page invites the family to pray together and identify ways in which they can be open to receiving God's call in their lives.

S: The image of Jesus, smiling and extending his hands in a giving manner, welcomes the child and invites them to respond. The children surrounding Jesus are signing and gesturing the ways in which they thank God and what they thank God for.

R: Invite the child, family and loved ones to make a thank you card by filling the box with ways in which they join the children and thank God. You can extend this activity by sticking a photograph of a reader at Mass, reading from the lectern, and explain that this is how they thank God with their actions. They respond to a call like Samuel.

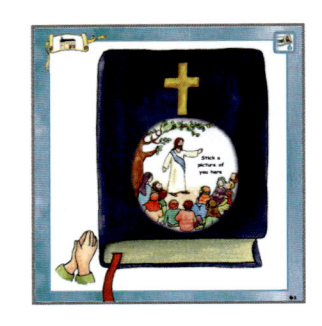

CHAPTER 7   BREAD TO OFFER

Page 64
You will need:
- Images of food made from bread. Be sensitive if the child has an allergy to wheat.

P: Within a catechetical programme for children with intellectual disabilities, it is important that the child is able to distinguish between bread that is eaten every day and the bread that is changed in substance – transubstantiated. This page helps the child to visually experience how a substance changes and how they consume the changed product. It shows how the ingredient of wheat is part of making bread and part of something that people eat.

S: The page shows the process of wheat turning from seed to end product. The image of the road should now be familiar to the child and should be linked to their journey towards a special meal. The idea will be to enable the child to link the image of wheat to bread, to consuming the bread. You should also highlight the concept of somebody having to prepare the bread as this will invite the child to make links with the substance of the Eucharist in the chapter.

R: Invite the child to interact with the story by recognising and naming pictures. Invite them to place an image of their choice of food that is made from wheat or food that they might share. Highlight that the food began from a seed and the sun that God gave to help it grow.

Page 65
You will need:
- Images of people who help the child and cook for the child.
- Images of the child helping or ways in which the child can help.

P: This page seeks to help the child to think about times when they share meals and to identify the preparation of food and their own individual role within it. It invites the child to identify a special celebration and place themselves and the person that prepares it into the circle.

S: The circle identifies a focus on "sharing a meal". The image used is the same as the child who receives in chapter six and, if possible, you should make this link. The image between the R boxes is there to help the child remember the concept of being helped and of helping. You may like to remind the child of this from previous chapters.

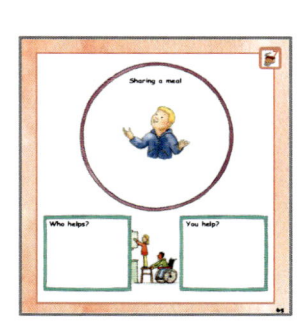

R: Invite the child to use the circle to stick pictures of, draw or represent a particular meal that is important to them. In the boxes the child should place the images of people who help them and the ways in which they help. In this way we begin to suggest the personal and communal contribution that is made when we share Mass and the Eucharist.

Pages 66 and 67

These pages tell stories to the children to reinforce the giving and saving nature of God.

Page 66
You will need:
- To follow the OSP.

P: This page tells the Old Testament story of the people led by Moses who were hungry and fed by God. The speech bubble states that "God saves" and can draw upon the work done on this area earlier in your journey.

S: You can use the images in the box to help share the story. The simplified words for the story could be:
"Moses was in the desert at the burning bush [link with chapter 5]. God spoke to him again. Everyone was hungry. Moses asked God about his promised land, he asked for help; God gave everyone special food."

R: The empty box should be used to encourage the child to ask/ communicate a question or identify the moment that God gives to or saves the people.

Page 67
You will need:
- To follow the OSP.

P: This is the story of the feeding of the five thousand, from the New Testament. The speech bubble continues to present the saving nature of God but shows that, in the New Testament, it is the actions of Jesus that save. The purpose of this page will be to enable the children to share in the way the people wanted to be with Jesus, how they placed their need before him, and how he asked God to help him provide for God's people.

S: The picture in the box will help you to tell the story. The words could be:
"People wanted to be with Jesus and receive his words. The people were hungry. A little boy had some bread and some fish. Jesus took the food and offered it to God. The five loaves and the two fish fed lots and lots of people. It was amazing."

R: You should now be familiar with the communication and processing skills of the child. Invite them to make a response to the story and to express how they feel. Use the R box for their response.

Page 68
Invite the child to be creative with this page. You could make a copy of the fish and the loaves and the child could place them in Jesus' hands. Alternatively they could place an image of some food of their choice.

Page 69
You will need:
- To copy the small images of the Bible, hosts, chalice and offertory bag (top of page).

P: The purpose of this page is to help the child move from the Liturgy of the Word to the Liturgy of the Eucharist and to identify their place within the Mass. It introduces them to the rituals that take place. The images and actions of this page should enable the child to identify the preparation of the altar for the gifts and the prayers that surround this action.

S: The page shares the image of an offertory procession with people bringing the gifts to the accessible sanctuary and altar. The characters have empty hands. Some of the characters in the procession are from previous chapters and you may like to explore this as they have accompanied the journey so far

R: Using the long empty box at the centre of the page, invite the child to place a photograph of the Eucharistic procession in their own parish. Help the child make the link to the moment in the Mass that this page seeks to present. Using the cut-out symbols from the page, invite the child to stick them into the hands of the people in the procession. You could extend this by inviting the child and their loved ones to take up the gifts at Mass and you could take a photo of this event and use it to make the link in the R box.

Page 70
You will need:
- To copy the three images from the boxes and invite the child to place/stick the images on the altar.

P: This page now begins to link the substance of the Eucharist to the everyday experience of the child and help them to understand how the gifts are brought to the altar and offered to God the Father.

S: On this page we begin to share information with the children about the link between the altar, the body of Christ and the gifts that are offered. So that it links to the offertory procession on page 69, we maintain the image of the altar. The large image of Jesus with his arms open represents the body of Christ offered. Below, the three boxes hold images of the hosts, the chalice and the wine, and the paten. This is so that the child can make a link to the wine brought in the offertory and the chalice that holds it. The gold box holds an image of an empty paten onto which the child can make a personal response from their life.

R: Invite the child to place the three gifts onto the altar and explain what the gifts are each time the child places one onto the altar. Highlight how the giving hands of Jesus are giving us the gift of himself. Use the words at the top of the page to help you.

Page 71
You will need:
- Photographs of the child using their gifts, engaging in everyday activities, laughing or using hobbies to help others.

P: This page shows how God receives all the gifts that we share with love and that God's heart is big.

S: The receiving hand of God helps the child to know that God receives our gifts with love.

R: Using the heart in the same way that you would circle communication, invite the children to place a photograph or an image of themselves into the large heart of God. This action will represent the child offering their gifts to God and will make a consolidating link to previous pages.

Page 72
You will need:
- To follow the process for using lotto games: copy the lotto game and make matching cards.
- To extend: use photograph of matching symbols and actions from the Mass.

P: This page seeks to help the child consolidate and revisit the themes of the chapter and the elements of the Eucharist that they have explored thus far.

S: The lotto game holds six gifts and is linked to the "Holy, Holy". The image, along the bottom of the page, is another procession. This time it is of people singing "Hosanna". The procession is led by Jesus on a donkey and the people follow, showing how much they love and support him.

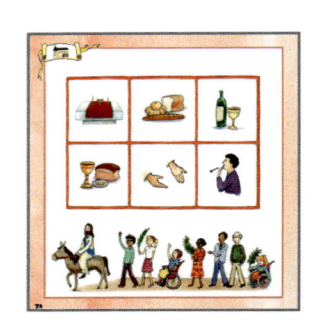

R: Invite the child to use the lotto game as in past chapters and say/sign or sing the "Holy, Holy" to the child as gift. You can extend this activity by inviting the child to match the symbols in the game with some "real life" matching photographs from the Mass. Encourage the link between the processions here and on page 69.

Page 73 Family time
You will need:
- Images of food or moments for which you want to pray and thank God. These images can reflect those on the outside of the circle.

P: This page helps the family to explore how God created the world and filled our lives with gifts, including the gift of Jesus.

S: The prayer border is made out of grapes and wine, bread, the sun, wheat, rain and the world. In the middle of the circle is the child receiving the gifts that make the bread and the wine. You should place pictures of these or an image of someone saying thank you, from previous chapters, into the circle.

R: The R box has praying hands in, for the family to make a prayer of thanks.

Page 74
This page is self-explanatory and encourages the family to make some bread, so as to make a direct link with the journey of the wheat from page 64. The child should now be familiar with the road image and so it is hoped that it will form a direct link and a visual way to experience a change of substance from flour to food.

NOTES

CHAPTER 8   FRUIT OF THE VINE

Page 76
You will need:
- Copies of the grapes on the vine from this page.
- Photographs or names of people who help them to feel God.

P: This page helps the child to engage with Jesus' saying: "I am the vine and you are the branches." For a child with intellectual disability this is a very difficult concept as they cannot imagine Jesus, who is a person, saying he is a tree. For someone who processes language logically, this will not make sense. We have therefore changed it so that the child is able to engage visually in these words of Christ.

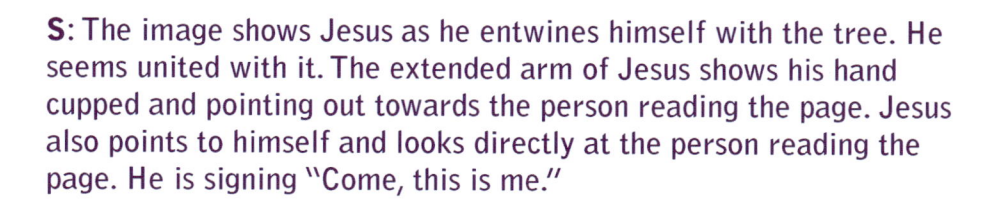

S: The image shows Jesus as he entwines himself with the tree. He seems united with it. The extended arm of Jesus shows his hand cupped and pointing out towards the person reading the page. Jesus also points to himself and looks directly at the person reading the page. He is signing "Come, this is me."

R: Invite the child to match the fruit and stick their own bunch on each branch. Ask the child to show you who helps them to feel God. Invite the child to stick small photographs or names of people they choose on the fruit.

Page 77
You will need:
- Copies of images of grapes.
- Copies of images of people working from page 75.

P: This page links the workers in the vineyard, found on page 75, with the making of wine through the sacrifice of their hard work. The page uses circle communication as with previous chapters.

S: The images of a jug and a wine cup help the child to see that wine comes from grapes and that the wine is made by people (use the picture on page 75 to help share this fact: the work of the people is an explanation of a liturgical reality). The words "What makes good wine?" should help the child to give an answer.

R: Invite the child to fill the two empty R boxes with photocopies of the grapes and people from page 75.

Page 78
You will need:
- A copy of the image of the jug and grapes from the R box on this page.
- A photograph of people in the parish bringing up the wine to the altar.

P: This page aims to link the making of the wine to that offered at the Mass, to the work of the people and to Jesus as the substance of the wine.

S: Using circle communication and an image of the altar, we begin to see a shift from the focus on the Liturgy of the Word to the Liturgy of the Eucharist; this is represented through the image of a Bible on the altar and an empty space for the gifts to be added. In the left-hand box below the circle you will find the symbols that will be placed on the altar to mark this shift.

R: Invite the child to place the image of the wine onto the altar in the circle. Place the photograph of the parish offertory in the circle and help the child to identify the process of offering the wine (fruit of the vine, work of our hands, offered up to God).

Page 79
You will need:
- A photograph of the child.

P: This page helps the child to child see that the offertory at Mass is the work of the people. It also begins to build an understanding that God gives us the gifts and we take our gifts to God. God protects us.

S: The page shows an image of the people in the vineyard and also a large "blessing hand" of God. On the hill, the prophet Isaiah's arms are outstretched. You should make a speech bubble and write the words "God's promise". Say these words to the child and point to all the beauty of the page.

R: Invite the child to place their photograph among the workers so as to identify themselves as someone whom God uses and needs as his worker in the vineyard.

Page 80
You will need:
- To follow the OSP.

P: The purpose of this page is to help the child know the story of the wedding feast of Cana and how Jesus made a good change, bringing good news to the family. It is also a link to the concept of the wine that changes in substance from previous pages.

50

S: The story is simplified in a way that helps the child see the change of substance as a good change that brings good outcomes to the celebration of the people (thus making the link). The words will help share the story.

R: By now you should be familiar with the skills and communication processes of the child. Use the R box to help them respond to the story.

Page 81

P: This page seeks to present a way of consolidating and finishing the story from page 80.

S: In the top right-hand corner of the page we find the giving hands of God showing the "changed wine" and we see Jesus signing "It's ok now".

R: Encourage the child to respond by pointing to the emotions that occurred as Jesus changed the wine at the wedding feast. Invite the child to change the colour of the jug. They can also sign "It's ok now".

Page 82
You will need:
- Images of party food and drink.

This is an activity page that aims to allow the child to consolidate the catechesis from the chapter. Encourage the child to be creative and to fill the table with party food. Let them share the story again if they wish to.

Page 83
This page is catechetical and will enable you to support the child's consolidation of catechesis from this chapter.

P: The page enables the child to see that the body of Christ brings together past, present and future.

S: The large image of Jesus has three boxes spanning the width of his body. The hands of Jesus hold and embrace the boxes in a gesture that brings them together. Thus the images in the boxes form the trunk of his body. This has a direct link to the way in which his body is entwined with the tree on page 76. Between each box the links symbolise the unity and connection. This page begins, therefore, to make links with the image from the beginning of the book, where the child begins the journey to the Eucharist with Jesus. The three boxes represent the way in which the workers of the past, the celebration of the people in the present, and the promise of eternal unity with God, are all found and held together in the body of Christ.

51

Page 84
You will need:
- Images of whatever the child may want to share with Jesus or thank God for.

P: This page gives the child the space to thank God for Jesus and for anything they may wish to express from their journey so far. They have had to link a lot of theological metaphors and messages in this chapter – this page allows them to stick pictures of what they want to thank God and the life of Jesus for.

S/R: Using circle communication we will combine the sharing and the response for this page. In the circle Jesus is held in the hands of God and he is identified as being at the centre of all our praise and thanks. This will begin the concept of receiving Jesus from God and of Jesus offering his life to God. Encourage the child to stick in an image or photo of what they wish to thank God for.

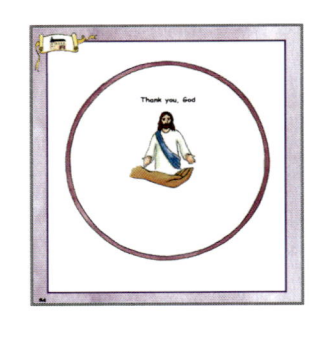

Page 85
You will need:
- To copy the images in the lotto game and make matching cards.

This lotto game aims to help the child consolidate and recognise the main symbols and movements within the Eucharistic act. Jesus is the one that gives the gift of himself. Invite the child to interact or to match images.

Page 86 *Family time*
You will need:
- Images that match and fit inside the empty spaces on the page.

P: This creative activity page will allow family and loved ones to help the child to recognise God's created world by seeing the image of a world in the giving hands of God.

S: The words "Blessed is God who gives… Amen" leave space for family prayer to be created.

R: The children are invited to fill the empty images in exactly the same way as the children in *I Belong*.

CHAPTER 9   DO THIS IN MEMORY OF ME

Pages 88 and 89
These pages encourage the child to match images from their own life to the meals in the picture. This is to help them have a concept of a shared meal.

Page 88
You will need:
- Images from the child's life that reflect those shown in the boxes.

P: The page invites the child to identify the differences between certain types of meals and occasions. This is to reinforce the special nature of the shared meal found in the Eucharist.

S: The boxes hold images of differing occasions and different types of food that we eat for each different occasion.

R: Invite the child to place matching images from their life where they are eating or sharing different occasions or different food.

Page 89
This is a creative activity. You should invite the child to create an image of their choice.

Page 90
You will need:
- To follow the OSP.

P: This page relays the story of the Passover and links it to the Last Supper, showing both as special meals.

S: The images share the story of the Passover and the Last Supper. Suggested text for the story of the Passover meal:
"God told his people he would give them a wonderful land. God told them to eat quickly and to travel to the land. They ate a special meal. God showed them where to go."
The image of the story shows people eating the Passover feast. You can interact with the images of the people eating hastily, with bags ready to go. This image of people doing something inside a venue is a direct link to what we do in church from the early chapters of this programme. God's leading hand, outside the door, leads them to freedom. The meal happened just before the people went away to the promised land.

R: The empty communication boxes allow the child to order the story.

Page 91
You will need:
- To follow the OSP.

P: This page relays the story of the Last Supper; and it is in the exact same format as the Passover meal. This is to show the vital unity between the two stories and how they are the promises of God: God's covenants.

S: The images share the story of the Last Supper. The simplified story should be:
"Jesus went to a room to share a special meal. He said, 'This is my body, this is my blood. I give it to everyone so that I can always be with you.'"
The image shows people eating the Passover feast but also uses images from the Mass. Highlight that this is a new special meal and that it is wonderful. The feast happened just before Jesus gave his life on the cross. God's leading hand, outside the door, will help you to explain that Jesus gives himself so that we are free and happy.

R: The empty communication boxes allow the child to order the story.

Page 92
You will need:
- To copy the images in the speech bubbles.
- Your own images of a priest with chalice and host.

P: This page helps the child make a visual link with the story of the Last Supper from the previous page. Your aim is to help the child see that the words we share in the Eucharistic Prayer were words spoken by Jesus but that these words result in an action.

S: Using circle communication, encourage the child to notice the image of Jesus from the Last Supper with his hands extended and ready to hold something.

R: Invite the child to place the speech bubbles on either side of Jesus within the circle. This identifies the words belonging to Jesus. Stick a photograph of the priest offering up the gifts, from the child's parish, in the R box.

Page 93
This is a creative activity page that invites the child to decorate and to stick their own photo in so that they too are called to the table with Jesus.

Page 94
You will need:
- A photograph of the child.
- A copy of the images in the communication boxes of this page.

P: This page makes a very strong link with the title page of the *I Belong Special* book that showed the child that they are on a journey towards union with Jesus. This page now shows the image of Jesus in the Eucharist with the child. The aim is to help the child see that the same love from the heart of Christ comes to us as we receive the Eucharist that is changed into his presence in our life.

S: On the image of Jesus you should draw a heart. Place the image of the gifts in the middle box. Share with the child: "The love of Jesus is in the gifts of the host and the wine. It is changed like at Cana. It is given to you with love."

R: Invite the child to stick their own photo in the top right-hand box. The idea is that the child places their response in line with the love that comes from the heart of Christ. Encourage the child to use the R box for anything more that they may wish to express.

Page 95
You will need to:
- Follow the process for the lotto games.
- Copy images to make matching cards.

P: The purpose of this page is to help the child revisit some of the catechesis they have encountered.

S: The lotto game allows the child to match cards and revisit themes.

R: Invite the child to use the R box to place a photo from their personal experience or of the parish at the Eucharistic table.

Page 96
You will need:
- Images for which the child may want to give thanks.

P: This page introduces the rosary and takes the form of circle communication, inviting the child to give thanks for people in our life who share themselves with us like Jesus does.

S: The symbol of the rosary will help the child know that it is a prayer about the life of Jesus. In the middle of the rosary is a picture of Jesus

R: Invite the child and their family to fill the circle by placing the names and images of people whom they wish to thank. In this thanksgiving circle the people they pray for will be present to Jesus and Jesus will be present to them.

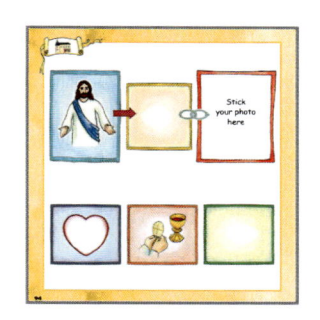

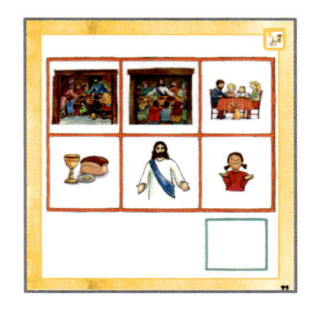

NOTES

NOTES

CHAPTER 10 BODY OF CHRIST

This chapter seeks to highlight the very nature of the Eucharist and the change that it makes to our lives. The chapter highlights the concept of change as something positive and life-giving.

Page 98

P: This page is purely informative and helps you to show how things change from one thing into another and that the changes are positive and life-giving.

S: The page shares the story of the change from the frogspawn (original substance), to the tadpole, to the frog (new reality) and in the same way, from the caterpillar to the butterfly.
The thumbs-up image with the words "Life changes" in the middle of the two images will help you to explain this reality to the child.

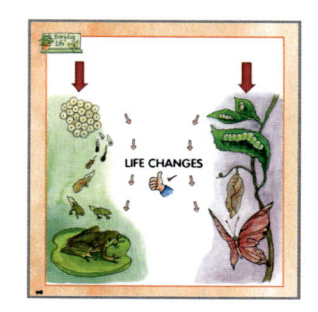

There is no response to be recorded on this page.

Page 99
You will need:
- A photograph of the child when they were a baby.
- A photograph of the child as they are in the present.

P: The purpose of this page is to help the child see how things change and become beautiful and how this links to their life.

S: The communication boxes give space to the child to identify how they themselves have grown and how they are the same person when they were a baby as they are now.

R: The feeling strip allows the child to express how they feel. Invite them to use the emotions to express their feelings about who they are and how they have grown. The words across the top of the page read "I am the same person." This will help you explain and link to page 98.

Page 100
You will need:
- To follow the OSP.
- Images of people or drawings of people walking away with their back to the cross.

P: The purpose of this page is to link the road from the Last Supper to the death of Christ on Calvary (link with chapter 9).

S: The New Testament scripture strip shows a speech bubble with the words "I give my life". The image of Calvary is the same as on page 91. The words for the story should be:
"Jesus died on the cross. His friends were sad. They thought he had gone for ever. But the story did not end at all."

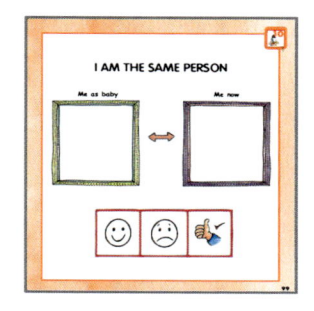

Give the child some photographs of people walking away and place them on the hill. Alternatively you could draw this. Explain to the child that the people think that Jesus is gone for ever and this will make sense of the empty cross.

R: Use the R box to allow the child to order the story.

Page 101
You will need:
- To follow the process of the lotto game.
- To make matching cards.

P: This page continues the story that has not ended. It joins the story of Mary Magdalene, who recognises Jesus, and the disciples on the road to Emmaus, who recognise Jesus in the breaking of the bread.

S: The two strips of three boxes tell the stories.
Text for the first story:
"Mary did not find the body of Jesus. Jesus came to Mary. Jesus said 'It is me. I am alive!'"
Text for the second story:
"Two disciples were sad, they missed Jesus. Jesus came to them. They ate together and the disciples knew Jesus was with them."
The strips are encompassed by two arrows that link to the pages about life changing (pages 98-99). This shows the story from when it begins to the positive outcome of the encounter with Jesus.

R: Invite the child to match images from the story and to trace the arrows if they can. Highlight how a sad situation changed into a happy one… and that Jesus is always with us – a great outcome!

Page 102
This is a creative activity page for the child to enjoy.

Page 103
You will need:
- Matching images from a real-life Mass.

P: This page makes the link between changing realities (from not recognisable to recognisable, as in previous pages). The page seeks to link up: the offering of the priest and the people; the giving of Christ in the Eucharist; and the realisation that, as Jesus signs in Makaton, "This is me". It is Christ we receive.

S: The page shares moments from the Mass where a change occurs from one reality to another. The arrow shows how it is all linked and what happens is a positive encounter with Christ. The arrow seeks to show that, as with the previous pages, the change that occurs is life-giving and the life that is given is Jesus; the offering of the priest in the visual symbol of bread and wine becomes Christ present and shared among us.

R: Invite the child to place a matching photograph from their own Mass into the R box.

Page 104
You will need:
- An image of the child on their First Communion day.
- A copy of an image of Jesus from the *I Belong Special* book.
- Images from the Mass and the Eucharist.
- Everyday images.

P: This page allows the child to see how the Eucharist is something that helps us in our everyday life.

S: Using circle communication you should share examples of how receiving the Eucharist can be linked to everyday experiences.

R: As the child prepares to receive the Eucharist, invite them to Makaton sign "thank you". In the middle of the circle, make a picture of Jesus and add a photo of the child on the day of their first Eucharist. Invite the child to place pictures or photographs of them doing everyday activities. Over the top of the circle highlight the blessing hands of God. Encourage the child to use the empty R box to create their own prayer.

Page 105
You will need:
- Images that represent the actions and objects that are named in the lotto board.

P: This page invites the child to consolidate through doing a lotto game with a difference. It helps them to recognise the symbols that they will encounter each time they receive the Eucharist.

S: The lotto game shows the words "Good Friday, Special Mass/Easter, Tabernacle, Sanctuary Light, Body of Christ, Blessed Sacrament". This activity encourages the child to make their own lotto game and become familiar with the sound of church symbols and terms.

R: Invite the child to place the matching images of the words in the boxes. You may have to help them. To extend this, you could make matching lotto cards from photographs of real-life objects. You could also visit the church and allow the child to touch the relevant objects and symbols, and then place the images into the boxes.

Page 106

This is an invitation for the child to make and give to people that they wish to invite to their special sacrament. We have left a space for them to put photos of the people they wish to invite. In this way they take ownership of their day and of this life-giving event in their life.

CHAPTER 11   TO LOVE AND TO SERVE

Page 108
You will need:
- Images of food and drink that the child likes.

This is a creative activity page which enables the child to explore how food and drink is important for our growth and is an everyday thing.

Page 109
P: This page helps to link the spiritual experience to the lived-out physical one. It aims to help the child join up the "everyday" and the "communion" experience.

S: The difference between the two is displayed in the images on this page that show actions and their consequences.
- Row one: The girl in the image is hungry. The arrow leads to the consequence of her eating food. She feels full because the food helps her live.
- Row two: The girl in the image holds out her hands ready for the Eucharist. The arrow leads to the consequence of her receiving the Eucharist. She is bursting with joy, having received all that she needs to live life to the full and to have a happy spirit.

R: The feeling strip allows the child to show their feelings about the different concepts of body and spirit.

Page 110
The circle communication page is the same as in chapter 6 with the Bible in the middle of the circle (page 58 of *I Belong Special*). Be creative and choose to share a scripture story of your choice. By now you will be familiar with the child and how they receive scripture. The words on this page read "More stories about Jesus".

R: Invite the child to place images or words in the circle in response to the story if they wish to.

Page 111
You will need:
- Photographs of the child in church, with others or alone.

P: This page links the family praying together, the child praying alone, and space for the child to express what they may like to do as a member of the community. It is about new life in the Eucharistic community and about having a place where they belong.

S: Each praying situation is within the arms of Christ. The child in the wheelchair is signing "I give myself" and facing the person of Christ.

R: Invite the child to place an image of how they would like to give themselves to Christ and to the parish community. The R box is named "Me in my church". Joining the boxes together are large praying hands. Help the child to develop a deeper sense of service and belonging within the parish community.

Page 112
You will need:
- An image depicting how the child shows God to others.

P: This page helps the child to show thanks and praise to God. The letter will help you make a letter for their prayer sponsor. It will be a letter of thanks.

S: The page is filled with the image of an envelope. In the middle of the envelope is an image of a child signing "thank you".

R: The communication boxes show images from previous chapters of two friends helping one another and the sharing of a meal. Invite the child to use the R box to complete the picture by placing an image of their choice which explains how they show God to others. Once the page is collated, make a photocopy of the communication boxes and turn it into a letter for the child's prayer sponsor.

Page 113
You will need :
- Images from the child's First Communion day.

This is a creative activity page, using circle communication to help the child share anything they wish to about their First Communion day. Encourage the child to be creative and to use images from the day.

Pages 114 and 115
These pages are self-explanatory and should use photographs as well as words.

I do hope you enjoyed the journey of *I Belong Special*. Thank you for all your creativity and sharing.

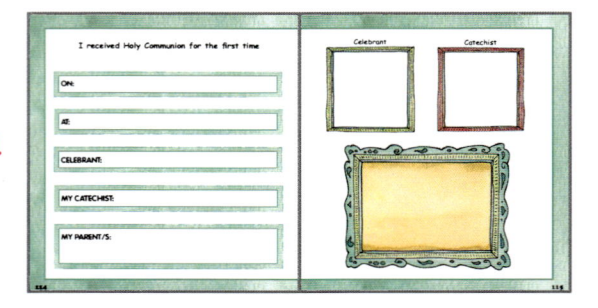

Contacts
The Kairos Forum www.abdn.ac.uk/kairos-forum
The Makaton Charity www.makaton.org
Email: info@makaton.org
Tel: 01276 606760